BEHOLD THE FRONT PAGE!

BEHOLD THE FRONT PAGE!

Robert Moore, Jamie Buckley
and Nick Newman

MAINSTREAM
PUBLISHING

First published in Great Britain in 1993 by
 MAINSTREAM PUBLISHING COMPANY (EDINBURGH) LTD.,
7 Albany Street, Edinburgh EH1 3UG.

ISBN 1 85158597 4

A catalogue record for this book is available from the British Library.

Printed in Great Britain by Butler and Tanner Ltd, Frome, Somerset.

to tim

blessed are the cheesemakers

OLD

TESTAMENT

NEW/s INTERNATIONAL VERSION

I MADE AND EARTH IN 7 DAYS

Astounding claims by bearded one

ASTONISHING new claims about how life started have been made by a self-styled creator of the universe called God.

The almighty allegations proclaim that the world was NOT formed over thousands of millions of years – but in a week-long creative spectacular.

Abracadabra

OUT goes Evolution. **IN** comes the Seven-Day Theory.

The heavenly hypothesis is sure to raise eyebrows amongst boffins and education chiefs. But last night God was unrepentant. Here's how he pulled it off:

■**DAY ONE**: GISSA LIGHT! The Lord said "Let there be Light!" and there was. He divided it from the dark and called them Day and Night.

Howzat!

■**DAY TWO**: HEAVENS ABOVE! That swirling mass of hydrogen and oxygen we call the atmosphere was whipped up at the snap of his fingers.

■**DAY THREE**: LAND AHOY! Two fingers to the theory of continental drift - God parted the land from the sea in just 24 hours.

■**DAY FOUR**: I'M GOING TO MAKE YOU A STAR! Long before Hollywood, God was making stars of his own. He invented the Sun and the Moon too.

■**DAY FIVE**: FISH YOU WERE HERE! Still full of ideas, Our Father filled the oceans with "beasts of the sea" and the air with "flighty fowl".

■**DAY SIX**: JUMPING JEHOVAH! The master magician didn't just pull rabbits out of his hat, he produced every living creature that walks upon the earth - including *us*!

Barking

■**DAY SEVEN**: PUT YER FEET UP! Knocking up a sustainable eco-system in less than a week is no mean task.

God gave himself the day off and called it the Sabbath. And he told us:

"Hereafter, do the same!"

THE BIBLE SAYS ...

IT'S a creation sensation!

All things bright and beautiful, the Lord God made them all – *and that's official.*

Top god God has made a perfect planet in less than a week – and put *us* in charge.

Thanks your holiness! It's safe in our hands!

HEAVEN

"I can't even get him to put up a set of shelves."

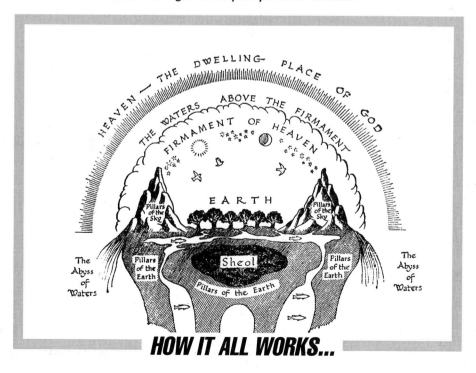

HOW IT ALL WORKS...

10 things you need to know about God

GOD... He even invented marijuana

1 He doesn't have any parents, but he's everyone's Dad.

2 God spelt backwards is Dog.

3 He can giveth life and taketh it away.

4 Likes: The Pope, clap-happy evangelicals, and people who don't ask too many questions.

5 Dislikes: Charles Darwin, Albert Einstein, and the bishop of Durham.

6 He has a flair for creativity – look at giraffes.

7 No-one knows why He invented wasps.

8 He's dead keen on the environment.

9 He can sometimes be a bit holier than thou.

10 He's watching you as you read this.

WOULD YOU ADAM AND EVE IT?

❶ Adam was the first human to walk this earth - he was made out of mud and came to life when God blew up his nose.

❷ The prototype primate's first job was to think up names for all the animals.

❸ But when God told him to find a mate from amongst them – our fussy forefather didn't fancy anything.

❹ So top doc God made Eve out of Adam's spare rib in a 12-hour miracle operation.

❺ The passionate pensioner was 130 years old when he had his third son, Seth. And the original sinner lived to a Bible-tastic 930.

❻ All mankind is descended from Adam and Eve – all 6 billion of us. Luckily in-breeding was not a problem.

ON YER BIKE!

Eviction for mankind's Mum and Dad

Before the fall everyone was friends in the Garden of Eden

EARTH'S first couple are to get the boot from their paradise love-nest after feasting on forbidden fruit.

God has **banished** Adam and Eve from the Garden of Eden after they broke their vow not to eat apples from the Tree of Knowledge.

And the Golden Crunch came last night when the let-down Lord found them under a bush, wearing fig leaf G-strings.

Strange but true

ONCE they were the couple who had it all - the penthouse of paradise homes "like something out of The Blue Lagoon".

NOW the good life is over and they're set to live on stony ground.

And it looks like they've ruined it for the rest of us too.

Under the strict terms of their lease paradise's perfect couple were ordered to walk "dumb and naked like beasts of the field" across all of Eden.

"Eatest freely from any tree in the Garden but not of the trees of Life or Knowledge, located somewhere in the middle," God told them.

But trouble flared when easily led Eve, 19, made friends with a four-legged snake.

One thing lead to another and the smarmy serpent soon tempted Eve to stray into the no-go areas and taste the fruit. Then she used

By BIBLE REPORTER

her fulsome 36-26-36 charms to lead her own hubby down the garden path.

Oops!

After one bite the new-age naturists both realised they were naked and "blushed readily". And when they heard God walking through the almighty arboretum, they hid in shame.

At first the cowering couple denied it all, but God – who is all-knowing, all-being, and all-seeing – wasn't having any of it:

● **Cursed!** be all snakes to lose their legs and crawl upon their bellies.

● **Cursed!** be all women to give birth with sorrow and be ruled by their hubbies.

● **Cursed!** be all men to walk upon thorns and thistles and sweat for their suppers.

"Now get out!" he **stormed.**

THE BIBLE SAYS...

YOU SILLY COW!

Us blokes were doing fine till you came along, Eve.

Now we've all got to work for a living.

We might have known it would be a woman who'd muck things up.

Women! Can't live with 'em, can't live without 'em!

BIBLE BABES ARE RIPE FOR PICKING

★ Apple corrr! We wouldn't mind a taste of Eve's forbidden fruit! And she's certainly got a nice pair. But you won't find any apples left in the Garden of Eden - she's Adam all.

★ Curvy Eve, 19, might have mucked things up for mankind when she fell for Satan's saucy serpent. But we think you'll agree, showing off her fig-leafed figure is the best way of apple-ogising to the Bible readers!

IT'S ALL GOING HORRIBLY WRONG

GOD'S PIPE-DREAM for a perfect planet is fast turning into a nightmare after his fledgling first family have plunged themselves into a bloody feud.

The fatal fracas arose when Adam's sons were asked to come up with harvest-time offerings.

Cain knocked together some "fruits of the ground", but Able whipped up the "firstlings of his flock and the fat thereof". But Cain's load of old crop failed to meet BC standards for divine donations.

And God's subsequent snub sparked off a sacrificial showdown which ended with Cain killing Abel in the corn fields.

Cereal killer Cain thought he was in for a Biblical bollocking – but the Lord, in his wisdom, showed mercy.

Sinning

"If any man kills you, he will be killed himself – **seven times over**."

This latest drama will be seen by God watchers as a further blow to the Almighty's pet project for peace on earth.

And the lamenting Lord admits

By BIBLE REPORTER

he might have made some mistakes. "I'd imagined something like *Little House on the Prairie* – but it's beginning to look more like *Crimewatch UK*," he told *The Bible*.

Critics are already calling for a review: "We blame the parents for this breakdown of family values. Once *they* start sinning what hope is there for the kids?"

Any hopes God had for an early retirement may now be shelved as he heads back to the great big drawing board in the sky.

YOU THE JURY

■ Was God right to let Cain off for the cold-blooded murder of his innocent brother?

■ Or should the Lord have hurled him into a pit of burning snakes?

■ Or perhaps you think God didn't have much option – seeing as how Cane was the only human being left alive.

RING *THE BIBLE* AND GIVE US YOUR VERDICT: 0898 123456

WARNING

HUMANITY HEADING FOR HOLY HIGH-JUMP

SOURCES close to God claim the big man is losing patience with mankind's miserable antics.

Close friends warn that Our Father is falling into a deep depression over the state of the world.

"He's getting very cynical and keeps talking about ending it all!" they told *The Bible*.

Oo-err

In a statement issued this morning, God stormed "I have seen that man is weak and of the flesh. His wickedness is great upon the earth."

And the hot-tempered Holy One vowed to wreak revenge. "I will destroy man whom I have created and every beast and fowl and creeping thing that creepeth on the earth."

***The Bible Says*: We've really gone and done it now – page 6**

FLOODY

GUTTED GOD did the unthinkable last night and punished the wicked by drowning the whole world.

The let-down Lord submerged the Earth in a massive monsoon.

Rain stops play

And the only people to be saved were 651-year-old Noah and his ageing offspring – whom God had simply described as "good".

The Old Testament's favourite family were tipped off in advance and told to build a massive house-boat that would hold two of every beast, fowl and even insect.

Thre hundred cubits long and 50 cubits wide – it was always going to be a squash.

But DIY fanatic Noah never doubted he could do it - even when passers-by mocked him for building a boat in the middle of a desert.

Floating voter

And Noah had the last laugh when the flood finally came.

But it wasn't all plain sailing. The holy soul survivors endured 40 days and 40 nights of typhoon torment before the rain ceased.

And they spent a further 150 days holed-up in the house-boat before it came to rest on Mount Ararat.

Noah's first bid to find land was not an instant success. He sent

Why weren't we told?

From Our Bible Correspondent

forth a crow – not a bird known for its homing qualities – and never saw it again.

But he struck it lucky when he pulled out a dove. And after several nail-biting hours the bird returned bearing an olive leaf.

Fowl play

Seven days later the waters withdrew. It was the moment they'd all been waiting for!

And God proved he was in the party mood too, by telling every man, beast, fowl and even insect to "Go forth and multiply!"

---

20 THINGS YOU DIDN'T NOAH 'BOUT THE ARK
page 6

page 6

THE BIBLE SAYS...

GOD MUST GO!

You can't drown everyone on the basis of a few minor outbreaks of naughtiness!

A written warning is one thing – but wiping out the whole world on a whim is not on.

That is the action of a madman.

And not what we would expect from an all-loving Lord.

Of course our flesh is weak – but that's part of the fun of life!

BIBLE

† NAUTICAL NOAH lived to be an impressive 950 years old before finally popping off to that great ark in the sky. It was a good innings for the old sea dog, but his last couple of centuries were spent in a drunken haze as he tended his vineyard.

SPOT

Life's always better in The Bible...

HELL!

Bible Fun   **by newman**

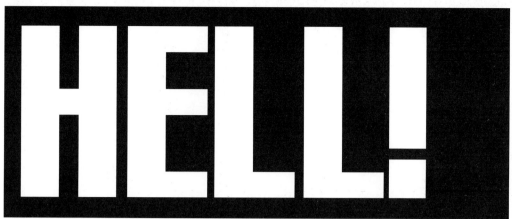

"Did we have to bring two rottweilers?"

"Really, Noah, that sort of thing went out with the... er... um..."

The Holy Book that gives you:

A bit of this...

PANDA BORN IN CAPTIVITY

■ THE birth of 8lb Chi Chi caused delight amongst the eight human beings left on Earth.

...a bit of that...

LEMMINGS GO OVERBOARD

■ NOAH has expressed deep concern about the behaviour of the lemming species which kept jumping ship. "That's no way to evolve," he told them sternly.

...and a bit of the other

PAINT THE WHOLE WORLD WITH A RAINBOW

■ GOD last night proved he was man enough to admit that he might have gone too far.

He didn't actually say sorry in so many words – but the colourful creator *did* produce a rainbow instead.

And that is being widely interpreted by God watchers as a guilt-edged guarantee that he won't do it again.

THEY'RE AT IT AGAIN!

THE mud's still wet but mankind is already knee-deep in no-good nonsense. For the citizens of Babel are building a giant tower.

Their aim?

To erect a stairway to heaven and snatch a sneak preview of the Pearly Gates.

Get off-a my cloud

But God isn't having any of it. He sees the pesky plan as an invasion of his privacy. "It's a monstrous carbuncle!" he has told close friends.

And before the devious developers could even finish the plumbing. God threw a spanner in the works by suddenly making everyone speak in different tongues. It left people quite literally babbling in Bablyonia.

On-site negotiations at once collapsed as workers downed tools in several languages.

Maastricht

"One minute we're all going round chatting like old mates," an eye-witness complained. "Next thing you know, half of us are speaking gobbledygook,"

"Jakali dweeb um gower coca cola," added a confused Canaanite.

TOWER OF BABEL ... "unfinished folly"

PHWOOOR! WAHEY! COOOR!

BABEL DEVELOPMENTS

"The workmen still have a common language."

TOP JOB
SHOCK FOR
UNKNOWN
SHEPHERD

A CHILDLESS seventy-five year old has been hand-picked by God to become the father of his number one nation.

Opportunity knocked for ageing Abraham when he was chosen from hundreds of Hebrew hopefuls to start off the Chosen People.

The Lord told him that all of Canaan would one day belong to his kids.

Small print

But the heavenly hand-out has come with a catch. For God also told Abraham that the seed of his loins was destined to be:

■ **strangers** in a foreign land,
■ **enslaved** for 400 years, and
■ **suffer** many hardships in the name of religion.

"Seventy-five may be a bit late to start a family – let alone a whole nation – but I'm going to rise to the challenge," said the sprightly septuagenarian.

BIBLE

✝ WHAT a surprise-aac!

Abraham and wife, Sarah, both in their early hundreds, had almost given up hope of bearing a child.

But now they too will hear the patter of tiny feet.

God has blessed them with a son, called Isaac.

SPOT

Speech bubble: NOW THAT'S WHAT I CALL THE EARTH MOVING!

Sign: SODOM

SOD 'EM ALL!

FIERY FATE FOR CITIES TWINNED IN SIN

THE PARTY'S over for the sex-fiend fetishists of Sodom and Gomorrah – for God has melted them with fire and brimstone.

God *had* offered to spare the evil oasis after Abraham revealed his nephew, Lot, lived there.

And he sent in two angels to see if they could find "just ten good people" in the two cities.

Scorched earth policy

But the mercy-dash mission got off to a bad start when a gang of kerb-crawling Sodomites took a shine to the divine delegation.

The sicko citizens made a bid to bed the winged wonders - and would not even stop when Lot offered to trade them for his two virgin daughters.

"It wasn't a good move," admitted one of the fiends as he found himself blinded.

And the cheesed-off cherubs immediately called off all hopes for salvation.

They gave Lot two hours to round up his relatives and flee the land as fast as he could.

Then they tipped off the Lord who unleashed a whirlwind storm of burning sulphur which rained down upon the cities.

Sulphur the little children

No one escaped the Almighty's acid attack. He burned the cities, "and all the plain, and all the inhabitants of the cities, and that which grew upon the land."

"It was a complete write-off," said a singed passer-by.

It's a Family Affair

Lot's daughters hide a guilty secret. For the scheming sisters once got their old man drunk and then both *knew* him – *two nights on the trot*!

Lot insists he was out cold at the time, but now the fertile father has unwittingly spawned two whole tribes: the Moabites and the Ammonites.

> **■ BIBLE**
>
> **† Cheeky** Lot's wife couldn't resist a final peek. She broke God's no-looking-back rule and found herself turned into a pillar of salt!
>
> **SPOT ■**

ANOTHER SELF-RIGHTEOUS EXCLUSIVE

WE PROBE SEX SHOCK SCANDAL

NOTHING could prepare Bible investigators for what they saw in the sex-den cities of Sodom and Gomorrah. Things not fit to print in a family holy book.

It left them shocked and deeply traumatised.

Sod's law

For daily life in the Soho of the Sahara is an orgy of sun, sea, sex and sangria - a place where just "knowing" someone means having **full sex**.

"Marriage is for wimps and girls exist only for sex," admitted one self-confessed pervert. "And so do sheep, come to that," he added.

One scantily clad female even offered to **begat** our reporter's child. He declined.

MORE SINNING ON PAGES 3, 4, 5, 6, 7, 8, 9, 10, 11, 12 & 13

BIBLE OFFER

Win our SODOM SEX VIDEO and see the sinning for yourself!

DIAL THE DIRT-BUSTERS

☐ Do you live in a village of vice?
☐ If so, *The Bible* wants to know.
☐ Call our crime desk *now!*

THE BIBLE SAYS... SULPHUR's too good for them.

It's hard to believe the depths to which some depraved degenerates will sink.

But sinning must be nipped in the bud – wherever it's found. And the sick souls of Sodom are set to spend the next few centuries in hell.

It's the best place for 'em!

EWE LUCKY BASTARD!

INFANT Isaac faced a biblical barbecuing last night –*from his own dad*.

But the tiny tot escaped being sacrificed when an angel of the Lord conjured up a ram that would do instead!

Bon appetit

Abraham had been instructed by the Lord to make an offering

By Bible Reporter

of his only son. So the forlorn father tricked his son into thinking they were going for a three-day holy fast-and-feast.

But picnic turned to panic when Isaac found out *he* was on the menu!

And the death-bid dad was on the verge of slitting his son's throat and striking the match when an angel of the Lord stepped in with an amazing eleventh hour reprieve:

"Hold your pyre!" he shouted. "You've passed the test of faith.

"Taketh this instead - that you may eat," he added, pointing to a conveniently appearing ram caught in a nearby bush.

Cherub champ … in the nick of time.

ESAU YOU COMING A MILE OFF!

GULLIBLE Esau fell for the oldest trick in the Good Book yesterday, and saw the title of "God's Chosen One" slip through his hands.

Not only did hairy-man Esau trade his birthright for a measly bowl of soup.

He also missed out on his father's inheritance.

Cunning stunt

And it was all thanks to his kid brother Jacob who:

■ **DRESSED** up as a goat.

■ **FOOLED** their foggy-eyed father Isaac into thinking *he* was the bristly brethren!

The hair-piece hoax was hatched by pushy mum Rebecca in a bid to snatch the family fortune from clumsy eldest son Esau.

Bottom-of-the-class Esau was last night tearing his hair out as panic-stricken Jacob fled to Mesopotamia to stay with his uncle Laban.

LAUGH AT OUR BIBLE FUN PAGE

page 38

LOOK OUT FOR GREAT BIBLE TV

page 42

BIBLE WOMAN

COOKING:

- How to feed 5000 and still have enough for a casserole

- **Eve's apple-pie – a recipe you'd sin for**

- **Fast-food tips from THE SPUD-U-LIKES**

FASHION:

- Is it chic to be a Shamenite?

- *WEAR YOUR HAIR LIKE A MOABITE*

- **Win a date with the Up-ALL-Nites**

NEXT WEEK

IS YOUR HUBBY A WANNA-FIGHT?

How to get pregnant by your old man – Lot's daughters

Serves you right !

Leah … not veil-y nice

Rachel … utter babe

MARRIAGE MIX-UP FOR JOKE FAN JACOB

PRACTICAL joke mad Jacob soon got his just desserts.

For he suffered seven years hard labour before his uncle Laban would allow him to marry favourite daughter Rachel.

But when the big day finally came, loopy Laban pulled a stag party stunt and swapped redhead Rachel, 18, for ugly elder sister Leah, aged 38!

With all the veils, Jacob couldn't tell the difference and he found himself hitched to the Hebrew horror.

Then laid back Laban forced Jacob to sweat for seven more years before finally bedding his intended.

But it was worth the wait and the bigamist believer made up for lost time by breeding like a Rabbite.

Leah gave him *nine* Israelite infants - all of whom turned out evil.

And Rachel gave him two: the pip-squeak prodigies Joseph and Benjamin.

I SHOULD SO

★ **From herder of goats to wearer of coats!** Now you can read my true story – only in The Bible

★ **Read** how I was a lowly herder of goats!

★ **Discover** my slumber-time super-sense!

★ **Wince** as I stood accused of rape!

★ **Cringe** when I suck up to the screws while doing porridge!

★ **Hear** how I won Pharaoh's favour with inside info on the grain markets!

★ **You too** can have a déjà vu. Read my book and share my success!

Chapter One

IT'S NEVER easy being a youngster in a family of eleven brothers — especially when you're as gifted as me.

It was uncanny, but from the age of three I knew I was better than everyone else.

In fact I was so popular I couldn't see why my brothers hated me so much. But hate me they did.

Mind you, I didn't do myself any favours by boasting about my dreams which were tipping me for the top. My favourite trick was to wind them up each morning with another annoying anecdote…

Chapter Two

IT WAS my father's gift of a ready-to-wear rainbow-sleeved reversible that really got my brothers shirty.

For them it was the final straw and before you could say full-length-trouser-suit I was bundled into a slimy well.

Less talented people might have given up hope. But right there and then I vowed to kiss goodbye to the sleepy suburbs of Canaan and head for the bright lights of Egypt and the Heliopolis high-life.

Which was just as well because the next thing I knew, my own kith and kin sold me into slavery and I was carted off to Cairo by a hairy bunch of Ishmaelites.

I later learnt that my back-stabbing brethren ripped up my jacket and convinced Dad that I'd been devoured by a nondescript desert beast. I'm prepared to forget the pain they caused him, but I'll never forgive them for ruining my jacket.

Chapter Three

ARRIVING IN Cairo was something of a shock - smocks were out and tunics were in. I barely had time to raise my hemline before being taken to market.

It wasn't hard to stand head and shoulders above the hoi polloi chained either side, and I was soon discovered by a palace talent scout.

Work as a slave was not exactly creative, but I had all the yashmaks a girl could want - *and* I was rubbing shoulders with eunuchs and minstrels. I had to laugh – if only my bumpkin brothers could see me now!

Chapter Four

I QUICKLY wormed my way into boss-man Potiphar's good books. But problems started when I refused to worm my way into his wife. And when I refused to become her toyboy lover she accused me of rape. *Moi!*

No one would believe the word of a humble slave - or a pretentious one for that matter - and her hoodwinked hubby had me hurled into jail. My dreams of fame and fortune lay in tatters.

But Lady Luck soon smiled on her favourite son when two prisoner pals were panicked by the *same* vexatious vision in their sleep. I hedged my bets and told one he'd be freed and the other he'd be in for the chop.

Oh happy day! I was right. My reputation quickly spread far and wide within the walls of Potiphar's penitentiary and soon I was voted Person Most Likely To Succeed by my fellow inmates.

# of a day-dream believer ...

BE LUCKY

THE THINGS I DIDN'T DREAM

- that my brothers would throw me into a well
- where religion would get the world
- that my life would be turned into a block-buster musical and I wouldn't see a penny

NEXT WEEK:
How I wanted to be a supermodel

Chapter Five

THEN CAME the break I'd been waiting for. Pharaoh himself had been troubled by tossing and turning. I was immediately called up for a bedside brainstorm.

I listened patiently as Pharaoh told of seven fat cows he'd seen come out of the Nile to be eaten up by seven skinny ones!

Quickly dismissing the possibility of a mad cow plague - I decided it could only mean we were in for some pretty topsy turvey weather.

I told Pharaoh the same - and he immediately gave me a seat on his right hand. And what a firm, authoritative hand it was.

Chapter Six

I'D TAKEN a gamble but my predictions paid off and I was soon proclaimed Chief of Famine Relief.

I simply yielded myself up to the almighty forces of fate as promotion after promotion was thrust upon me.

Then the governor's post came up for grabs and I grasped it firmly. Before you could say grain mountain, I'd sold enough over-priced stock back to the punters to make myself a very rich man indeed. I was the toast of the Old Testament, and fondly hailed as the dandy of the desert wherever I went in my spectacular short-sleeved shrouds.

Chapter Seven

QUELLE HORREUR! My brothers arrived in town - dressed like something out of another testament!

And let's face it, it doesn't do a governor any good to be seen with a bunch of nomadic deadbeats.

Luckily they didn't recognise me and I had them grovelling at my feet as they begged for food to save their starving families back in Canaan.

But I was in no mood to talk about the good old days when I remembered what they'd done to my multi-coloured coat. And I decided to give them a taste of their own bully-boy medicine.

I told them to bring forth my father's favourite, young Benjamin, and I stitched him up by planting a golden cup inside his baggage.

Then I had him charged with theft. The silly goose almost passed out when I sentenced him to life in jail!

Only when they sobbed on my sandals did I reveal my true identity and send for the whole family at a Surprise! Surprise!-style tear session.

I gave them all the grain they could eat and we all lived happily ever after.

MOSES' MUM IN BULRUSH RAP

THE mother of Home Alone baby Moses was last night slammed by social workers for abandoning her only child on the river bank.

If it hadn't been for a kindly nurse, the two-month-old toddler would surely have perished.

But now the miracle tot is looking forward to a bright new future as Pharaoh's grandson. Talk about a lucky break!

My life of shame

MAN-OF-THE-PEOPLE Moses hides two guilty secrets.

For when he was a mixed-up adolescent the prophet-to-be murdered two Egyptian guards.

"They were smiting my brother Israelites," he confessed. "And I just snapped. But Pharaoh got wind of it and I had to up and leave."

I BABBLED WITH A BURNING BONSAI

MOSES has told how a happy hike up Mount Sinai changed his life when he ended up being heckled by a hedge!

He was tending his uncle's sheep when the small shrub burst into flames and told him to take off his shoes.

Then the flaming fauna revealed how Moses was tipped for the top. In a firework finale the babbling bush ordered him to leave his flock and free the Chosen People from Pharaoh's evil clutches.

You too can hear the voice of God - ring:

0898 1234567

MILITANT MOSES RUNS AMOK IN PHARAOH FUN-PALACE

'On yer bike, Israelite' – Moses told

TROUBLE-MAKING union boss Moses is up to his dirty tricks again, claim Pharaoh insiders.

The top level flare-up occurred between the loony left-wing leader of the Israelites and the Egyptian premier after they failed to reach agreement over the great pyramid-building strike.

In a stormy meeting Moses:

● **Threw** down his staff and turned it into a snake.

● **Struck** the Nile's water and turned it into blood.

● **Unleashed** a plague of frogs and flies.

● **Cursed** all livestock with a nasty strain of Mad Cow disease.

● **Cast** boils across the land.

● **Hurled down** hailstones upon the people of Egypt.

● And, as if that wasn't enough, he rounded it off by **plunging** Egypt into three days of darkness!

"He was really angry," a close friend confided.

Let my people go-go

But furious Pharaoh, 9, refused to step down and free the slaves. And as negotiations reached deadlock Moses, 80, pulled out his joker: *his Archangel Gabriel!*

In a daring SAS-style raid, the holocaustic holy ghost swept across the land killing every firstborn "be it man or beast". Only those who'd daubed their doors with the special †-mark were spared.

Flock off

This morning, in a dramatic U-turn, Pharaoh told Moses to "Up and leave Egypt!" adding "Take your flocks and herds too."

The rebels were last seen heading into the desert.

MOSES ... militant.

TOMORROW

How I parted the Red Sea

THE BIBLE SAYS . . .

Oi Pharaoh! That'll teach you for not playing fair-o!

We're not going to be pushed around by some tin-pot dictator. If you ask us, the Lord let you Egyptians off lightly.

Next time we meet an evil bunch of unbelievers, they'll wish they'd been born in another Testament!

The Bible – the truth, the holy truth and nothing but the truth

Don't be a statistic in the first-born frenzy!

By simply dousing this cross in lambs' blood and pinning it to your door you too can rest in peace!

The Bible
The book that supports *Our Boys*

Your cut-out-and-keep Passover Passport!

Who could pass over an offer like this?

ONE OUT A
OU
ISRAELITES IN MASS EXODUS

'ERE WE GO! That's what Moses told his people yesterday.

Taking only the barest belongings and some jewellery they'd pinched from Pharoah, the Biblical back-packers headed for the land of milk and honey.

Let's Go
Holy Land

They were armed with little more than good faith and a guide book called *Promised Land On A Shoestring*.

But rebel insiders said the mood was bouyant as the new-age travellers hitch-hiked their way to happiness.

FERRY CLEVER

BAFFLED BOFFINS are trying to figure out how Moses pulled off an escape that even Houdini would have been proud of.

Stuck between the Red Sea and an army of angry Egyptians it looked like curtains for the Chosen People - until "Mozza" Moses pulled out his trusty staff.

With one tap from his mystic mace the mighty waters parted. And he ordered the holy hordes to hitch up their smocks and paddle to the Promised Land.

Sea you later

The close shave occurred after frantic Pharaoh woke up to the fact that life without slaves would be no picnic.

But Moses tricked the troops into chasing him across the Red Sea and they quickly got bogged down in the Biblical by-pass.

Then as the fleeing faithful from the opposite bank, the prankster prophet held out his hand and ordered the waters to crash back down. It was a complete wipe out!

"You should have seen their faces!" laughed a gloating Gaddite. "Those Egyptians were stuck up Shiite creek without a paddle."

UDDER DISGRACE

Chosen People in bovine balls-up

THE ISRAELITES were caught with their pants down last night when Moses found them *worshipping* a *golden cow*!

Moses had left his brother Aaron in charge of the chosen people whilst he climbed Mount Sinai for a date with the deity.

Cowabungle!

But while Moses thrashed it out with a burning bush, the Israelites switched gods and became followers of Mooo – a little known golden calf God.

The livestock lovers then spent the next 40 days at an all-night rave.

Rave in the nave

"One thing led to another," admitted one of the farmyard faithful with glazed eyes.

And the dairy devotees were in the middle of a steamy sex-and-sacrifice orgy when Moses walked

"Commandments were made to be broken!"

in with his guidelines from God.

The commandments were headed, "Ten Things You Need To Know About God's Will."

But the Lord's liaison was in no mood for fun. He gave his people the gold shoulder and in a wild fury he:

- **SMASHED** the top man's textbook tablets
- **RULED OUT** all future religious rodeos, and
- **CONDEMNED** the fringe-religion ravers to spend another 40

years in the desert and **miss out** on the Promised Land.

Bullish behaviour

Then the party-pooping prophet put 3000 of them to death. And he ordered the rest to *melt* the calf and *drink* the gold.

Ring-leader Aaron, however, got off with a stiff warning and yellow card.

God-watchers say the bovine balls-up is sure to set back Israelite-God relations.

THE BIBLE SAYS...

WE never learn.

God can't turn his back for two minutes and we're already melting down a jewellery and moulding false idols.

Heaven knows how we got picked as the Chosen People in the first place – but we were.

And it's about time we started behaving like it!

MOSES' DEATH SOURS ENTRY INTO LAND OF MILK & HONEY

MIFFED MOSES never made it to the land of milk and honey because God told him he must die – with only yards to go!

It was a cruel blow after years of wandering in the wilderness but the Lord allowed him to peek at the Promised Land from a nearby mount called Nebo.

Then the prophet passed away.

He was just 120 years old - a spring chicken compared with other Old Testament old timers.

His forlorn followers have begun a 30 day mourn-athon and predict much "wailing and gnashing of teeth".

"If we hadn't started larking about with that cow - we'd have been here years ago," admitted a contrite Israelite.

"Hi Land of Milk and Honey, we're home."

Dear Delilah

PROBS
GROWING UP IS HARD TO DO

Dear Delilah,

Our brother is turning into a pre-madonna. When he's not dreaming about being the tallest bale of hay, he's poncing round in some girlie coat that dad bought him.

Now he says he wants us all to bow down to him. If he doesn't stop soon – we'll sell him into slavery.

**Sons of Jacob
– a sheep farm**

Dear Sons,

Sibling rivalry is always hard when a parent treats one of you differently.

But instead of feeling threatened, try to understand his dreams.

You may live to regret selling him off – but then again – knowing the Bible's bizarre twists, you may not.

Dear Delilah,

My house is over-run with plagues.

One minute its frogs, then there's gnats, and blow me down if my taps don't start spouting blood.

Next thing you know my husband comes up in boils. He says it's all due to a curse from God. Should I believe him?

**Puzzled,
Cairo.**

★ ★ ★

Dear Puzzled,

I get quite a few letters about plagues from my Egyptian readers – and would normally put it down to the sticky weather.

But yours are beginning to look a lot more serious. My advice is start watching the Israelites more closely; if they start acting weird and slapping bloody crosses on their doors, make sure you do the same!

Either that or up your flocks and leave.

Dear Delilah,

My husband hardly seems to notice me any more, what with his 300 concubines and 250 other wives.

I saw him at the well last month but I can't help feeling the sparkle's gone out of our marriage.

Are we cursed by God?

I'm even thinking of having an affair.

**Housewife,
Heliopolis**

Dear Housewife,

Don't even think about it! Women get stoned to death for just flirting these days.

I'm afraid you've had the misfortune of being born in Old Testament times and you'll just have to grin and bear it.

CHILD OF AN IMMACULATE DECEPTION?

HAVE A GO

It took God and Moses forty days to compile the all new Ten Commandments, and look what they came up with!

If you ask me, they've all gone soft. The Nation deserves tougher measures than this to keep its unwashed masses in check.

★ ★ ★

I bet Adam & Eve can see the true meaning of the expression "ignorance is bliss", heh? Still it's easy to be wise after the event - especially if you've just eaten from the Tree of Knowledge.

★ ★ ★

Just as well Noah and his family got on well. If it had been me and my mad-cap lot, we'd've been at each others throats before you could say "All aboard!"

★ ★ ★

If God didn't like his people eating pork, then why did he invent pigs?

★ ★ ★

I know it's not very politically correct to say this, but I think God has been totally indiscriminate in dealing with the Egyptians. Come on, God - give 'em a break!

BLOW ME DOWN

HORN BLAST HELL FOR JERICHO

CRUMBS! That's what the people of Jericho said yesterday as their whole city was flattened by a terrifying toot from seven trumpets.

The Chosen People were under orders to conquer the land of Canaan – but no one had told the good folk of Jericho that theirs was the Promised Land!

Walls – I scream

Newly elected Chosen Chief Joshua was under pressure to pull off a miracle to match his mentor Moses.

But the rookie rabbi came up trumps with a cunning plan and a musical twist.

He marched his troops around the city for **six days** with priests and silent trumpeters taking the lead.

At first they were met with bemused looks from the care-free Canaanites. But on the seventh day the army stopped and let rip a big-bang blast from the brass ensemble.

It caught the Jericho army completely off-guard, many of whom had been expecting a more conventional form of warfare.

Nothing was left standing apart from a house owned by a friendly hooker called Rahab.

Baton bomb

But just as the citizens of Jericho began to sell copies of the *Big Issue* to each other, God's children stormed in and handed out some good Old Testament justice.

With barely a blink they slaughtered every man, woman, child and even family pet.

"Nothing lives in that city that was in that city therein," confirmed a cheerful Chosen One.

BIBLE

✝ ISRAELITE ACHAN was one Chosen Person who really let the side down. He took time out from the massacre to loot some gold and pinch a cloak.

For this shameful behaviour artful Achan, 34, was duly stoned to death and his family burned alive for being his seed.

SPOT

BIBLE

✝ THE NEXT thousand odd years were spent fighting, the Philistines, the Canaanites, the Elamites, the Immerites, the Gibeonites, the Tinymites and any other "ites" – who'd made the mistake of thinking that the Promised Land was their home, too.

SPOT

Come on girls! Get yourself a Page 7 slice of heaven

HANDSOME Samson is sure to set your yashmak alight. He may look like a bouffant buffoon - but his luscious locks are the key to his strength. But when this saucy Saducee isn't wantonly slaughtering innocent Philistines, he likes to spend time on the beach, spread out on his De-lilo! We can see why you girls voted our long-haired lover from the Lebanon "Top of the Crops"!

Absolutely Delilah-tful

DISHY Delilah, 18, is pretty handy with a pair of scissors, but she won't make a Sam-song and dance about it.

The flirty Philistine offered to give long-time lover Samson a cut and blow job - but he misheard and let her lop off his locks.

It put the coiffured killer in a Timotei tantrum and he brought a giant temple down on his head and shoulders.

But we bet our red-blooded Bible readers wouldn't mind letting this Old Testament teaser grab them by the short and curlies!

THE BIBLE SAYS ...

GOD knows what this story has to do with religion.

But it makes a nice change.

GOTCHA!

Round One KO for have-a-go hero David

By BIBLE BASHER

SEVEN-STONE weakling Dave "Boy" David KO'd Golan "Heights" Goliath last night in a sling-shot showdown that spelt defeat for the entire Philistine army. And the teenage shepherd did it all with a single pebble!

The desert dust-up was a classic finale to this year's Middle East Cult Religion League - where different tribes meet up and massacre each other in a bid to prove whose god is best.

And there was not a seat to be had in the valley of Elah as the two nations turned out to watch the pre-slaughter warm-up undercard.

In the red corner towered the Philistine's 25-stone super trooper giant Goliath - dressed in brass from head to toe and armed to the teeth.

In the blue corner stood the five-foot Chosen People's champ, David, in a sheepskin smock and brandishing a catapult.

There were nearly blows before the bell when Goliath called his pint-sized foe a "ruddy youth". In a feather-weight fury David slammed *him* back for being an "un-circumcised Philistine"!

"That was below the belt," fumed a front-row

"To be absolutely honest, we were rather expecting Goliath to win.'

David: tiny but tough

fight fan.

But Goliath could not match his puny opponent's piety.

And with God on his side David knew the fight was a fix - so he picked up a pebble and hurled it at the heathen.

It hit Goliath between the eyes and knocked him out cold. Then before the ref could finish the count, the tiny terror cut off his head.

When the Philistines saw what the chimp-sized champ had done to their hero giant, they immediately fled to the hills.

But the Israelites followed hot on their heels and killed all those they caught.

THE BIBLE SAYS ...

HAD enough Filthystines - or do you want some more? See page 6.

Holy roast!

Sauna trauma for prisoners of conscience

THREE holy men have been flung into a fiery furnace after snubbing a 90-foot golden cow.

Meshach, Shadrach and Abednego – known to campaigners as the Babylon Three– were detained at His Majesty's pleasure after refusing to take part in nasty King Nebuchadnezzar's false-idol knees-up.

Phew! What a scorcher

But although their

By BIBLE REPORTER

guards were burnt to a cinder, the three devotees emerged without so much as a sun-tan - after getting a visit from that nick-of-time angel of the Lord.

"It was a real-life living-hell," said Shadrach in an unlikely quote to *The Bible*.

"It just goes to show the power of prayer," he added.

NIGHT THAT I CHEETAH-ED DEATH

Daniel tells of lion den drama

BEWILDERED believer Daniel thought it was maul over when he found himself hurled into a den of starving lions - but he ended up as the moggies' mate!

He was thrown into the King's cattery after ignoring a 30-day nationwide ban on believing.

Dan-imal magic

But the feline frolic turned to farce when desperate Dan used the power of prayer and left the lethargic lions refusing to take the bait.

It was the purr-fect ending for Daniel.

He was immediately released and restored as the King's chief advisor.

THE BIBLE SAYS - "You're Dan-tastic!"

GIANT WHALE ATE MY HUSBAND

- claims Jonah's wife

A DISTRAUGHT wife has told of her hubby's horror at being swallowed by a large fish!

The digestive disaster occurred while Jonah, 34, was on the run from God - who wanted him for his merry band of elite prophets.

He was off the coast of Spain when the long arm of the Lord finally caught up with him.

"You're nicked!" boomed a voice from on high as the Lord unleashed a storm to shake him up. The sea-sick skiver

By BIBLE REPORTER

soon had second thoughts and confessed all to his shipmates.

They chucked him overboard where he was promptly swallowed alive by a whale.

It took three days of crawling to the Creator before Jonah's stint in the stomach came to a sticky end and the whale took a second look at his lunch.

"I've seen the error of my ways," admitted the press-ganged prophet last night.

The return of Jonah

HOW HOLY ARE YOU?

Are you holy enough to become one of the Chosen People? Try our quiz and answer the following questions to see whether you've got what it takes to please the Almighty and make it through the Pearly Gates.
We think you'll be holy amazed. (*Readers of other religions need not play – you're damned already!*)

1. Your neighbour is an unbeliever. Do you:
a) *wish him a nice day*
b) *try to convert him*
c) *stone him to death?*

2. You come across a burning bush. Do you:
a) *walk past*
b) *try to put it out*
c) *have a conversation with God?*

3. A voice in your head tells you to sacrifice your son. Do you:
a) *visit the shrink*
b) *feel guilty and bottle out at the last moment*
c) *fatten him up and invite a few friends round?*

4. You see a really bright star one night. Do you:
a) *wonder if there's life on other planets*
b) *point it out to your friends*
c) *follow it for a few thousand miles on the off-chance that you might bump into a suckling Saviour?*

5. You live in the middle of a desert and someone tells you to build a giant boat. Do you:
a) *ignore the fool*
b) *laugh and pretend you got the joke*
c) *raise the alarm, buy some wood, and round up two of every kind?*

6. Your fiancee is pregnant – but she says she's still a virgin. Do you:
a) *tell her to stop drinking*
b) *break off your engagement*
c) *rejoice and become a step-dad to the Son of God?*

7. Your husband is 75 and threatens to father a whole nation. Do you:
a) *laugh*
b) *put bromide in his tea*
c) *lie back and think of the Promised Land?*

8. Your elder brother looks set to inherit a fortune. Do you:
a) *wish him well*
b) *suck up and hope he gives you some*
c) *dress up in a goatskin and trick your father into thinking he's you?*

9. Your God doesn't pull off a miracle for three days. Do you:
a) smile and keep the faith
b) feel insecure and wonder what you've done wrong
c) melt down your jewellery and build a golden cow?

10. On the Sabbath do you spend your day of rest by:
a) *joining friends for a few gourds down the Lamb & Hatchet*
b) *keeping yourself busy – the devil finds work for idle hands*
c) *Lying in bed all day without lifting so much as a fig leaf?*

11. After 3 months your husband turns up on the doorstep and claims he's been swallowed by a whale. Do you:
a) *ask if he's been having an affair*
b) *tell him to go and have a bath*
c) *boast to your friends that you're the wife of a prophet?*

12. You bring down a hammer on your thumb and accidentally take the Lord's name in vain. Does it make you:
a) *feel better*
b) *say 5 Hail Mary's*
c) *start panicking and prepare for a gnat storm?*

YOUR RELIGIOUS RATING

Mostly A's:
Pathetic! You wouldn't last five minutes in the Old Testament. *Bible Tip:* Enjoy your riches on earth because you sure as hell aren't going to get them in heaven.

Mostly B's:
You've got good intentions alright – but you're nowhere near extreme enough. If you really want to win Our Father's favour you'd better start behaving a bit more irrationally. *Bible Tip:* After a short stint in purgatory, you'll probably get paroled to the limbo-land of heaven's suburbia.

Mostly C's:
Nice going – you make Mother Theresa look cheap! You're on a one-way ticket to the pearly gates and a seat at the Captain's table. *Bible Tip:* Keep it up though - for heaven has no room for slackers.

THE BIBLE IS THE BOOK THAT LEAVES OTHER RELIGIONS ON THE FRINGE

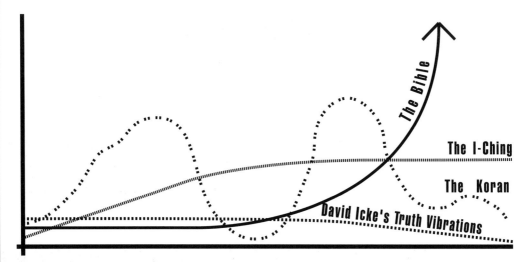

IT'S BAD LUCK for buddhists and maddening for muslims - but you can't call christianity a cult religion anymore. Your **Number One Bible** is tops with the teachers and pops with the preachers. And it's all thanks to *you* - our wonderful army of believers! In fact we're now so big we've started persecuting others. *So don't be a nerd - follow the herd!*

NEW TESTAMENT

THE GOSPEL ACCORDING TO ST RUPERT

VIRGIN ON THE

Phantom pregnancy for virgin housewife

A CARPENTER'S wife has given birth to the Son of God – and she claims that she is still a virgin!

Holy hormones!

The miracle birth took place after brunette bride-to-be Mary, 17, had a close encounter with the Holy Ghost. It was a genius gestation that left the young mum untouched.

Begetting is believing

But jealous boy-friend Joseph wouldn't believe that his pregnant bride-to-be had scored with the Lord so he broke off their engagement.

It took a visit from an angel to convince him it was true. The angel ordered Joseph to marry the Madonna but stay celibate till the birth.

This left no-times-a-night Joseph with nothing to do but sit down and choose a name.

Early suggestions like "Derek" were ditched and "Dwaine of Nazareth" didn't sound right either. But in the end they couldn't decide so God picked one for them.

"Jesus was the name chosen, and the name chosen was Jesus," confirmed a close friend of the couple.

"That Madonna will do anything outrageous for the publicity"

RIDICULOUS!

PINT-SIZED PROPHET IS SHEPHERDS' DELIGHT

"Smellies" always go down well at Christmas

Bathtime for baby Jesus

MILD CHILD Jesus was born in a pile of straw with a manger for his bed and a stable over his head.

Bethlehem's B&Bs were all booked up so Joseph and Mary had to make do with a stable.

The holy hovel was a humble beginning for the Lord's love child. But his divine delivery was witnessed by a complete cross-section of Middle East society.

Shepherds, kings, and assorted livestock all lined up to rejoice and pull stupid faces at the goo-goo guru.

Coochie coo

Three wise men even brought gifts of gold, frankincense and myrrh. The gleesome threesome immediately proclaimed the tiny tot "King of the Jews".

It was a precocious start for the pint-sized prophet.

HAVE A GO!

HOW irresponsible of those so-called "wise men" to give a toddler gifts of gold, frankincense and myrrh.

Not only are these presents difficult to play with, but they could be dangerous if swallowed.

BIBLE OFFER

ALL THIS WEEK WE'RE GOING CHRISTIAN CRAZY
● **Get away in a manger and win two weeks for three at a Red Sea resort!**

THE BIBLE SAYS . . .

OUR FATHER - he's top of the pops!

What a smashing way to start the New Testament. For just when we're all starting to flag – along comes God with a gift of his only son.

The weird birth was a nice touch too – that's sure to get him noticed.

He may be meek and mild - but the Sprog of Man will send us wild!

Like a virgin

BIBLE EXCLUSIVE

VIRGIN MADONNA has spoken exclusively to *The Bible* about her sensational fling with the Holy Ghost.

"It was like being touched for the very first time," she explained.

"He made me feel brand new," she added. "All shiny and new."

DELILAH  *Photo* CASEBOOK

Nine months ago my life was perfect. I'd met the girl of my dreams and we were soon to be wed.

Corrr! Look at the jugs on her!

I can't wait to get married.

But then I discovered she was pregnant- and it certainly wasn't by me!

What can I do! He'll never believe me if I tell the truth.

But one night I had an amazing dream

Blimey! It's an angel of the Lord!

Listen carefully! I will say zis only once. Mary is speaking ze truth. Marry'er and call your son "Jesus".

I wasn't going to fall a line like that, and we didn't talk for weeks.

Wait till I get my hands on the b*****d who ...!

Men! They'rs so immature.

Mary explained she'd been seeing the Holy Ghost - behind my back

Corr! Look at the jugs on her

Do you come here often?

I decided to give her the benefit of the doubt and now we have a wonderful baby boy.

But I can't help feeling I've been taken for a ride. What should I do?

Dear Delilah,

MY wife is pregnant but she swear she's still a virgin. She insists the child is the result of a particularly vivid dream she had about a "Holy Ghost".

I'd like to believe her but I don't want to end up a laughing stock.

Suspicious, Bethlehem

Dear Suspicious,

I'VE never heard this one before. Either you've fallen victim to an immaculate deception or you've got a Son of God on your hands.
Women say strange things when they're pregnant, but my advice is stick with her – you never know, your child may grow up to be a real leader of men.

PRICE WAR!

WHY BE A MUSLIM FOR £13.99 - WHEN YOU CAN BE A CHRISTIAN FOR £5.99?

OTHER holy books just can't compete with your big value £5.99 *Bible*!

Muslims are sure to miss out on Mecca when they buy the Koran for a crippling £13.99!

And the Bhagavad Gita is not much sweeter - Hindus must pay a horrifying £9.99!

Not much to meditate on there.

YOU CAN'T AFFORD TO MISS THE WORD OF THE LORD!

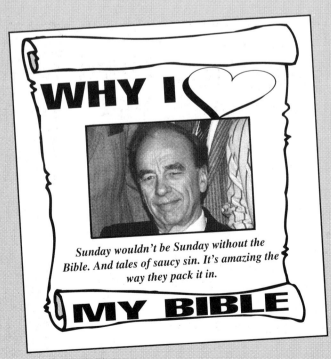

WHY I ♥

Sunday wouldn't be Sunday without the Bible. And tales of saucy sin. It's amazing the way they pack it in.

MY BIBLE

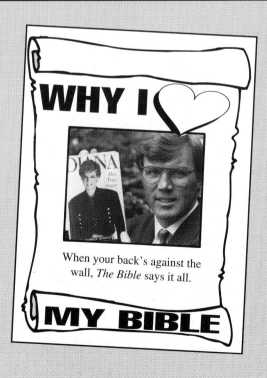

WHY I ♥

When your back's against the wall, *The Bible* says it all.

MY BIBLE

NAPPY NIGHTMARE

MAD DOG King Herod yesterday ordered the killing of all babies under two - after learning of the birth of baby Jesus.

The **BUTCHER OF BETHLEHEM** lost his rag after hearing how the Nazarene nipper was calling himself the King of the Jews.

Wonder

Herod had hoped to be tipped-off about his whereabouts from the three wise men who had witnessed the wonder-birth.

By OUR OWN REPORTER

But they had a collective dream in which God warned them not to meet the bloodthirsty beast.

So horrid Herod, 50, ordered his evil henchmen to set about the land and terrorise the under-twos.

But Joseph, Mary and their bundle of joy managed to flee the kindergarten catastrophe and escape to Egypt by donkey.

HEROD ... horrid

TOMORROW

TERROR TRAUMA OF TRAGIC TOT TRIPLETS

CULLING OF THE CUTIES

6 Rabid Facts About Mad Dog Herod

● HE counts pitbull terriers among his closest friends.

● SADDAM Hussein is one of his descendants.

● IT WAS *he* who started the region-wide craze for moustaches.

● HE avoids assassination by surrounding himself with Herod doubles.

● HE is building a giant super-catapult.

● EVEN Satan thinks he's evil.

HOW SAS WOULD TAKE OUT HEROD

○ **4.17am** THE conditions would have to be right.

○ **4.35am** THEN the team of crack troops would sweep in under cover of darkness and infiltrate Herod's elite inner circle. They are the only men in the world who can do the job.

○ **4.55am** ALL would don Arab beards and flowing head-dresses but some will be disguised as belly dancers. All would speak fluent Arabic.

○ **4.56am** HEROD could be sleeping with any number of his 154 wives - so it might-take some time to track him down.

○ **6.00am** ONE sling-shot is all they'd need to take out the tyrant. Barring that, a miracle would be nice.

○ **5.59am** BUT they'd turn up on the Sabbath and no-one would be around.

○ **5.38am** ALL would be captured by Herod's Republican Guard and eaten alive.

THE BIBLE SAYS . . .

SMITE HIM DOWN!

We've had just about enough of mad dog Herod and his baby bullying ways.

How can he be allowed to run around slaughtering innocents?

We know God works in mysterious ways - but there's mysterious and there's plain weird.

It's about time the Junta of Judea was taught a lesson he'll never forget.

10 FACTS TO GIVE YOU A HANDEL ON THE MESSIAH

- See page 10

Tiny teacher Jesus

Would you follow this man?

BAPTISM BONANZA FOR JESUS IN JORDAN

JESUS IS the new Messiah - and that's official!

Apprentice prophet Jesus joined his Baptist cousin John for a divine ducking in the river Jordan.

It was the religious rinse that gave Jesus the go-ahead to preach God's word.

At first John was reluctant to soak the Saviour, telling him

"I ought to be baptised by you!"

Speaking pigeon

But Jesus told him not to grovel for this was an order from up top.

By OUR MAN AT THE DUCKING

As the messiah was immersed, the heavens opened up and the sudden appearance of a pigeon surprised all - especially when they heard it speak!

"This is my beloved son in whom I am well pleased," declared the dove.

Such a statement coming from a bird convinced all that this really was the work of the Lord.

CART∞N

"Yes, eight out of ten big cats prefer it ..."

"There were rather a lot of cancellations after our first gig."

"What do you expect? It's a one-star hotel."

HEAVEN

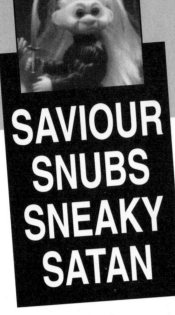

SAVIOUR SNUBS SNEAKY SATAN

JESUS FACED a battle of wits with Beelzebub last night - but came out on top and proved he was the Messiah with the mostest.

Too much of mom's cooking and a bar mitzvah too many had left the Chosen One chubby. So he'd taken 40 days off in the desert to slim down and prepare for the pressures of being a prophet.

But the Nazarene's navel gazing was interrupted when the devil arrived to have a dig at his divinity.

In a torrent of tempting torment he told Jesus to prove his "Son of God" status by:

● **TURNING** stones into bread and
● **JUMPING** off cliffs to be saved by angels!

But the 26 year old wonder-boy wouldn't bite on Beelzebub's bait and came back with a series of witty one-liners.

"Man shall not live by bread alone, but by every word that proceedeth out of the mouth of God," said the jocular Jew.

So Lucifer let rip with the offer of a lifetime:

"Worship me and the world will be all yours!"

But the Messiah was in no mood for messing and ordered Satan to "Get thee hence."

It was too much for bamboozled Beelzebub who promptly upped and left.

CALL OF THE MILD FOR DISCIPLE DOZEN

THE DO-GOOD DOZEN— that's what they're calling the twelve young men picked by Jesus to start his **ministry.**

"12"– THE NUMBER OF THE PRIEST

By BIBLE REPORTER

For they are some of the mildest men in the East.

And the merry band of disciples are fast winning fame for their many mild acts of meeknes.

Their preaching is sure to leave Buddhists bewildered and Hindu's hopping mad – but you early Christians are gonna love em.

For the "Preach Boys" have been blessed by the Lord and given powers to heal at a hundred paces.

KOOL AND THE GANG

HERE'S HOW Jesus rounded up his Maker's dozen while strolling by the shores of Lake Galilee:

● First he spotted two fisherman brothers - Simon, called Peter, and Andrew called Andrew.

"Come with me and I will make you fishers of men!" he appealed flamboyantly.

● Then he passed brothers James and John mending their nets.

"Come with me and I'll make you menders of men!" he proclaimed, stretching a metaphor.

By Our Reporter

Four became six, then six became eight, and so on - 'til the Christian cowboys stood twelve-fold strong.

"Once more unto the preach" was Jesus' command. But as the orthodox outlaws set off into the sunset, one called Thomas was heard to murmur "I'm not sure I'm really cut out for this."

Peter and Andrew ... they were just minding their own business

BIBLE

†JESUS has fallen foul of feminists after failing to pick any women. The would-be dungaree disciples have seen it as a snub and have even threatened to leave the church altogether.

SPOT

FAMILY FUN TO BEAT THE

JUNIOR BIBLE

REMEMBER KIDS: Just because *The Bible* has been proven scientifically and historically unlikely – **is no reason *not* to believe.**

+ + +

NEXT WEEK

WIN a weird beast! We all know that dinosaurs are just a bit of new-age nonsense – let's face it, not even God would think up something as daft as Diplodocus! But they're all the rage, so we're going to jump on the bandwagon too.

NOW YOU TOO CAN PLAY GOD!

Re-enact the New Testament with our wonderful set of disciple dolls

★ **JEZZA GENIUS!** Our Jesus doll has healing hands

★ **And springy feet for those sudden ascensions**

★ See Jesus do battle with the forces of darkness and save his pal, Peter, from the clutches of the evil Ayatollah.

● **You can hang Jezza from the ceiling in mid-resurrection pose!**
● **Or hold your own Sermon on the Mount!**

Collect all 12 and tease your friends who can't afford them!

PRE-BAR MITZVAH BLUES

GUIDE THAT TRIBE

Can you guide Moses and his people to the Promised Land?

Follow the routes and find out which path the Chosen People should choose.

Messing aboat on the water!

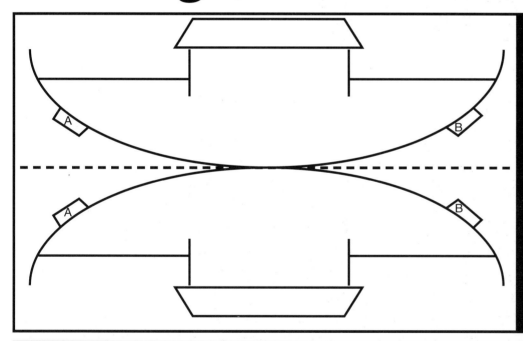

Hey kids! You all Noah 'bout the ark that saved us from total extinction – well here's your chance to build a replica and have a bathtime banjoree of your own.

Simply cut out the whole ship-shape, fold along the dotted line and lue A to A and B to B.

It's sailaway fun in yer number one *Bible*!

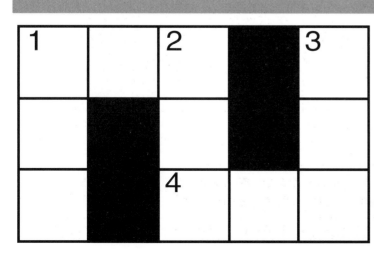

GOD'S WORD

ACROSS
1 Him upstairs. (3)
4 Sits on high with the son and the Holy Spirit. (3)

DOWN
1 This creator made a planet or two. (3)
2 Our canine friend. (3)
3 See 2 down spelt backwards for this Father. (3)

JESUS SPIKED OUR DRINKS!

HAPPY HEBREWS were found rolling in the gutter last night singing praises to our Lord! Their joy was down to Jesus who'd saved a wedding party from running out of wine.

The prophet pulled his plonk prank when the urns ran dry and disappointed diners began to kick up a fuss.

Bottoms up

But before the inebriated invitees could get too rowdy the Son of God stepped in to temper their spirits.

He announced a holy happy hour and turned the

By Our Reporter

water into wine!

Bloody Mary

His magnum effort certainly corked the attention of the guests who carried on celebrating into the early hours.

"All those that were there within were off their faces," admitted a hungover Hebrew later.

"Can you turn this English tap water into water?"

JOHN LOSES HIS HEAD OVER GIRL

THE SAVIOUR was said to be "seething" last night after hearing how his Baptist buddy John had been beheaded.

The disastrous decapitation took place during Herod's birthday booze-up, where the doomed deacon was being held captive.

Herod offered stepdaughter Salome anything she desired after the buxom belly-dancer delighted guests with a saucy seven-veil samba.

Prophet-eroless

But the dirty dancing star couldn't decide what she wanted until her ambitious mum stepped in with a bid for the Baptist's bonce on a plate!

Mum, Herodias, was still

BY BIBLE REPORTER

fuming after miffed minister John slammed her second marriage to Herod and snubbed the wedding. It was she who'd had the Baptist banged up.

Hubby Herod rather liked honest John, but he couldn't lose face in front of his friends - so he gave the order for the guillotine gaff.

When your back's against the wall, The Bible says it all ...

THE ALMIGHTY - HE'S ALRIGHTY!

Baptist At The Banquet

A plate for you to cherish

IT'S A story as sad as any told – immortalised for the first time on a plate skilfully brought to life by the loving hand of world-famous artist Lucas Cranach. His delicate use of shading, colour and texture perfectly captures the child-like innocence of sweet Salome. And hungry Herod can hardly keep his hands off.

As we gaze into it, we can almost hear the flies buzzing round poor John's head. And look at the glimmer of hope in those half-opened eyes!

Crafted in the finest clay, this once in a lifetime offer has been beautifully bordered with a 22-carat gilt edge – a striking effect that costs us almost nothing but makes the plate seem priceless. It's a plate to eat off *and* show off to your friends!

SATISFACTION GUARANTEED

Each plate is individually hand-numbered and accompanied by a Certificate of Authenticity. If you find this plate puts you off your food, too bad – you should have thought of that before.

RESERVATION APPLICATION

Please accept my reservation for this fine collectors' clay plate. I am a gullible old lady of over 80 and I happily accept your claims that this plate will be an investment. I understand I need SEND NO MONEY NOW but that I will be billed for £20 a month for the rest of my natural life.

SULTRY SALOME IS OUR DISH OF THE DAY!

AFTER winning the head of John the Baptist, slinky Salome proved she really is the queen of D-cupitation!

And this 16-year-old Bible beauty is certainly used to making heads turn.

But if she offers to do the Lambada, make sure you don't end up in her larder!

SAVIOUR'S SUMMIT GETS THE BIG THUMBS UP !

(Well from the meek, at least)

IT WAS standing room only when Jesus appeared on a hilltop outside Galilea yesterday and wowed the crowd with a soaraway Sermon on the Mount.

To wild applause from the enthralled throng, the people's prophet delivered his key-note speech with a package of promises he claimed would bring "joy to all".

But it soon became clear that the Messiah's manifesto was bad news for the rich – and there was not much on offer for middle-income earners either.

Then Jesus whipped the poor into a frenzy by telling them exactly what they wanted to hear: that one day they too would be rich and inherit the world! "Though probably not in this lifetime," admitted one analyst expressing disquiet over the "riches in heaven" clause.

Here's what the Saviour had to say:

● **The poor in spirit will get the keys to heaven.**

● **The meek will inherit the earth.**

● **And the pure at heart will actually get to see God - an impressive offer by any-one's standards.**

But the broad-sweeping new measures were met with some caution.

"This won't go down well with the Romans," whispered a nervous Nazarene.

And there was anger amongst the peacemakers after they were told they'd have to make do with simply being called "The Children of God".

BUDGET BREAKDOWN OF HOLY HAND-OUTS

What it means to yer average geezer in the Gaza.

The PURE-AT-HEARTS: Being good has certainly paid off for them.

They get a chance of a life-time trip to see God. (Though not 'til they're dead.)

The POOR-IN-SPIRITS: They won't be so down-in-the-mouth when they leave their hovel and pick up the keys to God's penthouse pad.

The MEEKS: They get the best deal of all - for they inherit the earth.

JESUS PLEASES WITH BUDGET TEASERS

NO CHANGE TO FAGS AND BOOZE

BLESSED ARE THE CHIC - SEE BIBLE WOMAN

The lesser-known Herman on the Mount

TOE JOB MARY

EMBARRASSING engravings have been handed to The Bible showing Jesus having his feet washed by a prostitute!

The shocking sketches were sent anonymously in a brown papyrus envelope and no payment has been made.

Some are not fit to print in a family Holy Book - but we think our loyal readers have a right to

BY BIBLE REPORTER

know the sordid details all the same.

Mary Magdalene made her pass at the prophet while he feasted with a friendly Pharisee called Simon.

In a bid to be forgiven, the holy hooker crawled under the table and washed the teacher's tootsies with expensive oils.

Then she dried his feet with her hair!

The scenes stunned fellow diners and brought furious frowns from the Pharisees. But amazingly Jesus would only smile.

When asked why he was not angry the mild-mannered Messiah took the opportunity to tell a complicated parable that no one really got.

German on the Mount

Vermin on the Mount

IT'S NOT JUST A FASHION! IT'S NOT JUST A FAD!
BUT EVERYBODY'S GOING BIBLE MAD!!

GET YOURSELVES A PROPER JOB

I'VE had enough of these so-called "Chosen People".

They do nothing but run around the desert all day, upsetting sheep whilst high on manna from heaven.

Most of them haven't had a bath for generations and few have any regard for people's property.

They seem to think they can treat the wilderness as their own!

Promised

They may claim to be heading for the "Promised Land", but some of us have got to live in the real world.

If Moses can't call a halt to their meaningless meandering, this scum must be wiped from the face of the earth - before they start trying to push this manna-stuff on our youngsters.

Chosen People! Who are they trying to fool? It's just a feeble excuse to take drugs and sponge off society.

NICE ONE GOD!

YOUR Old Testament was a classic. It had me gripped to my seat and gasping for more.

Now I can hardly wait for the sequel - Old Testament II. Or may I suggest calling it the "New" Testament?

By WOODROW WHY O'WYATT

THE VOICE OF REASON

THE TIMES THEY ARE A-CHANGIN'

IT'S about time God got rid of his white beard and crusty image. No wonder only old people go to church! Old fogeys like us must keep up with the Times. I listen to pop music for example.

MESSY MESSIAH

THAT Jesus should smarten up his appearance. Just what kind of example does he think he's setting to the young?

Never trust a man with long hair and a beard, that's what I say.

In my day, prophets were proud to be messengers from God - and dressed accordingly. These days it seems that any old Hebrew hippy will do. God can't be short of candidates. I, myself, am not doing anything useful at the moment - and I'm already widely admired for getting complex ideas across to the masses.

An apology

NEXT WEEK: I BLAME EVE

WE AIN'T FAKIN', WE DON'T EAT BACON!

THE PIGGER THEY ARE THE HARDER THEY FALL!

TWO THOUSAND pigs plunged to their deaths after they were entered by what witnesses claimed was a "lemming demon". Jesus, 31, sent the demons into the herd after evicting them from the body of a Gadarene man – who was clearly one bacon sandwich short of a picnic.

Mad about you

JESUS has become a hero to all those posessed by devils' vast armies of victims are following him around in the hope he will cast out their evil spirits. And the politically correct prophet never turns anyone away!

COD ALMIGHTY!

SAVIOUR SERVES UP FAST-FOOD FISH FEAST FOR 5000

GOURMET GURU Jesus whipped up a feeding frenzy when he knocked together a three course meal for five thousand with just five loaves and two fish.

The Messiah turned master chef after being followed into the desert by hordes of hungry Hebrews eager to be healed.

But the dopey disciples had forgotten to pack any lunch and it was left to Jesus to whip up the miracle menu.

Hasn't anyone heard of nouvelle cuisine

HAVE A GO

The Bible only mentions the 5000 who *did* get fed. What about the other 15,000 who didn't get a look in? I queued up for days but didn't get so much as a fried bread-crumb. *Angry of Achar.*

SECOND HELPINGS

HALF-BAKED EXCLUSIVE

JESUS PULLED off the same stunt a week later - but this time feeding a **mere** 4000 with an **unimpressive** seven loaves of bread and fish.

The poor encore was a big let down for all those who had gone along hoping to witness the same miracle performed with just two loaves and a pilchard.

IT'S A HOLY HEAL-ATHON!

EPISTLES TO THE EDITOR

Dear Bible,

How could God have invented light on Day One if he didn't come up with the sun until Day Four?

Doubting Thomas

Dear Bible,

I wouldn't like to be Jesus and have my birthday clash with Christmas. He probably only get presents once a year. Perhaps this is why he often looks so glum.

Thoughtful of Galilea.

Dear Bible,

Well done Old Testament! I love the way you treat sinners. None of this wishy-washy New Testa-ment nonsense. Burn them all! That's what I say. And their families.

Angry of Achar

Dear Bible

Who'd want to be Jesus - it might bring you extra privileges, but Saviour's are always having to shake people's hands and heal them. You can't even rest on the Sabbath.

Thoughtful of Galiliea

Dear Bible,

I was very interested to read your story about these "Chosen People". I would like to become one. so can you tell me how I might join?

Dear reader,
Sorry but it's all down to whose seed you come from. And whether or not your grandfather of 20 genera tions ago was Abraham.

Dear Bible,

Just who do these Aborigines think they are? They claim to have had peace on earth and spiritual harmony for the last 40,000 years thanks to their hotchpotch cult religion. Isn't it time we converted them all to Christ-ianity and put them in touch with the realities of life.

Dear Bible,

Come to think of it, how do we know *when* God made the sun, if man wasn't around until Day Six?

Doubting Thomas

Dear Doubting,

Because it's written.

Dear Bible,

A friend of mine said I could go round and covet his wife for a few hours while he was at the market. But before I got the chance, God came up with the Ten Commandments which forbids such practice. Is the offer still valid?

Frustrated of Philistine

Dear Bible,

I have obeyed the rule that I should not lift a finger on the Sabbath for all my married life. The wife does everything for me!

Dear Bible,

Call me a Tradition-alist, but those travel-ling "Israelites" are making a mockery of laws meant to protect decent folk.

Dear Bible,

Do you think God's got something against Egypt? I think his actions were a bit indiscriminate.

Meek of Mecca

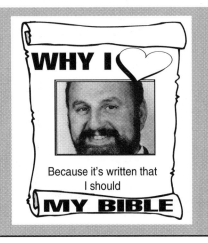

WHY I ♥
Because it's written that I should
MY BIBLE

WHY I ♥
When I'm confused about the news, my Bible tells me what to think
MY BIBLE

AMAZING FEET!

FUN-LOVING Jesus put the wind up his preacher pals yesterday when he walked on water!

The Messiah was on his way to save his mates from a monsoon at sea - but he couldn't resist playing a practical joke and left his boat on the bank!

The dumbfounded disciples mistook the surfing saviour for a ghost and "cried out with fear" until Jesus revealed his true identity. "Awesome dude," said Peter, who leapt overboard to copy his holy hero.

But the top disciple lost his nerve and quickly sank. He had to be hauled out by the fisher of men.

●**The Bible Says: Water Way To Go! – See Page 6**

GOD - HE'S THE HOLY GHOST-EST WITH THE MOSTEST

Sabbath - what a day for arrest !

IT WAS the miracle that backfired. A lame man was minding his own business begging in the temple when Jesus turned up and cured him.

"Rise, take up thy bed, and walk!" said the Saviour simply. It looked like just another run-of-the-mill miracle as the now fighting-fit fellow at once leapt to his feet.

But a gang of storm-

By BIBLE REPORTER

trooping Saducees arrived on the scene and immediately put the man under arrest for "carrying bedding on the day of rest". Then the finicky Pharisees had a go at Jesus too - and ticked him off for healing on the Sabbath.

But no-messing Jesus told the Jehovah jobsworths he could do what he liked because God was his Dad!

This claim has not gone down well with scribes and church elders.

Believe in God - it's the easy way out

VOTE PHARISEE

BECAUSE IT'S WRITTEN

DON'T BE A SINNER · JOIN THE WINNERS

JUST ASK JESUS!

NOT ALL of our readers can see the meaning of the parables as clearly as the Son of Man - but he's only too happy to shed light on the shady areas of his Prophetic policy. So, if you've got your toga in a tangle over one of the Messiah's religious riddles, then write in and we'll pass your letter on - he's only too keen to help.

Dear Jesus,

I'M A little concerned about the "eye of the needle" clause in your recent parable. I'm incredibly rich but I give a lot of money to charity. So what's going to happen to me come Judgment Day?

Dear Reader,

THIS ONE is always bound to upset the upper crust! What will happen is that you will be penalised according to a means test. The more you earn, the more you burn. But do not fret - lose a couple of pounds, you may still get through the eye of the needle!

Sorry, but you can't please all of the people all of the time.

Dear Jesus,

LET ME get this straight. In the parable of the Good Samaritan, we're supposed to stop our journey, at considerable inconvenience, haul some complete stranger to the nearest inn and pay for his room while he lounges around "recovering" all day.
Wouldn't it just be easier to be like the priest who passes by on the other side of the road.

Dear Jesus,

YOUR Parable of the Prodigal Son suits me down to the ground. Spend all your father's money on wine, women and song and when the shekels run dry, go back to Daddy to see if he'll up your allowance and have a bumper feast! Nice one, Jesus, we could do with more parables like this.

Dear Reader,

I don't think you've quite got it right, do you? Try standing nearer the front the next time you hear me speak.

Dear Reader,

NO. Look, let me start again .

Dear Jesus,

I DON'T understand *all* your parables - but they're great for keeping the kid's quiet on long journeys.

Dear Reader,

Yes - they have many uses.

Dear Jesus,

I'VE listened with interest to all of your parables, and may I say how clever I find them. But I've come up with my own parable which you may find interesting. It's called the Parable of the Lost Sock.

Dear Reader,

It's always nice to hear parables you make up -so send them in but do try and keep them to one side of parchment. (And no tablets).

Dear Jesus,

Did you here the parable about the Shi-ite, the Levite, and the Moabite.

Dear Reader,

All right – that's enough

● **Jesus would like to answer all your letters - but even with his team of disciple helpers, he cannot reply to everyone.**

HOLY BRAILLE!
BLIND MAN SEES

SEEING WAS believing for a blind man from Bethsaida when he was spat on by the Saviour and found his eyes immediatealy opened.

The man, who would not give his name, met the salivating Saviour on one of his whirlwind walkabouts and begged him to be healed of his faulty faculty.

Eager to please Jesus couldn't pass up the chance to try out his powers - so he spat in the blind man's face and placed his hands upon his eyes.

The Messiah's

By BIBLE REPORTER

mucus left the man with 20/20 vision and word quickly spread amongst the mesmerised multitude.

It was just the latest in a series of myopic miracles that have wowed the crowds but left the Pharisees fuming.

They have slammed the Messiah's mystical meetings and fear he might spark off copy-cat curings in nearby neighbourhoods.

"Before you know it every Tom, Dick and Herod will be going round gobbing at each other," one told *The Bible*.

THE BIBLE GETS THE **BIG** ONES!

I MADE HEAVEN AND EARTH IN SEVEN DAYS

Amazing claims of bearded Being

MILITANT MOSES RUNS AMOK IN PHARAOH FUN-PALACE

'On yer bike, Israelite' – Moses told

HOLY BRAILLE

Blind man sees

VIRGIN ON THE RIDICULOUS!

Pint-sized prophet is shepherds' delight

Our so-called rivals on *The Koran* have missed them all…

We broke the news that the universe was made in seven days. But they came up with some cock-and-bull story about it taking an unlikely six days!

Then we knocked them for six with our scoop on the Saviour. They took 500 years to come up with their Messiah – and even then they got it wrong. They thought he was called Mohammed!

THERE'S NO RIVAL TO YER NUMBER ONE BIBLE!

HOLY HALLUCINATION

JESUS JOINS PROPHET PALS IN 'TRIPPY' TRANSFIGURATION

AMAZED APOSTLES Peter, James and John were following Jesus yesterday when two top prophets appeared - *from beyond the grave!*

Prophet pals Moses and Elijah turned up on a mountain top to have a natter with the Son of Man.

It was the perfect setting for a classic Biblical head-to-head.

Dumbfounded disciples watched in wonder as Jesus turned a whiter shade of pale. Even his clothes shone "as the sun".

"It was a brilliant white," recalled Peter later. "Daz-ultra bright."

Although God did not make an appearance himself, He was represented by a big fluffy cloud!

The dazzled disciples were forced to hit the deck and hide their eyes.

By BIBLE REPORTER

"This is my own dear Son, with whom I am well pleased - listen to him!" spoke the Creator turned Cumuli Nimbus.

Then - as if by magic - the two Old Testament old-timers disappeared.

GRATEFUL DEAD

IT REALLY was the day of the living dead yesterday after super Saviour Jesus pulled off his biggest stunt yet - *and brought a dead man to life!*

Lucky Lazarus had been buried for four days and was well past his sell-by date when Jesus turned up at his tomb.

Thriller

There was wild applause from the watching crowd as Christ crept up to the crypt. All had high hopes of a holy happening - and perhaps an appearance from God himself!

But the Saviour simply commanded the corpse to "come forth".

Once again the Messiah's miracles brought gasps from the gob-smacked gathering.

Still feeling a bit woozy and smelling rather gamey Lazarus described his experience as "intense".

TAKE UP THY BED, AND LAMBETH WALK

"Oh no! It's the Pearly King of the Jews!"

BLACK MONDAY!

MONEY MARKETS were plunged into chaos yesterday after a top temple was raided ... *by the Son of God!*

Millions were lost as Jesus burst into the nave and overturned the tables – sending the shekels flying.

Financial flare-up

The moody messiah was said to have flown into a rage after hearing how the temple was being used for profit instead of prayer.

"He was one peeved-off prophet," admitted a haggling Hebrew.

"They may call him the lamb of God - but Jesus has proved you can't pull the wool over *his* eyes."

⬤**Shekel falls six points below Denarii!**

⬤**Sunday trading is banned too!**

MOODY MESSIAH IN TEMPLE TANTRUM

THE TEMPLE

"I've been done for insider dealing."

BIBLE MONEY

GET real Jesus!

You can't just storm into a temple and overturn tables – no questions asked.

Religion's all very well, but who's going to run the economy?

You're one kind of profit we can all do without.

VIEW FROM THE PULPIT

BIBLE BELTERS

YOUR TOP 10 IN TABLETS OF STONE

1
2
3
4
5
6
7
8
9
10

9.30 GOOD MORNING WITH JOSEPH & MARY: the Bible's favourite couple host another fun–packed show from their stable – looking at smock fashions for the spring and tackling the delicate subject of circumcision.

■ ■ ■ *Bible rating: It's what TV was invented for!*

10.00 KILROY! Are you possessed by devils?

10.30 SAINTS & SYNODS: the Bible soap pays another visit to the topsy-turvy world of church morality. In this episode Solomon cheats on four hundred of his wives.

■ ■ ■ *Bible rating: A real rave in the nave!*

11.30 JACKANORY: parables for pint-sized prophets.

12.10 GRANDSTAND: Exclusive coverage of Christians vs Muslims as the two religions battle it out to prove whose God is best. Plus updates on the weekend's stonings.

4.00 BLIND FAITH: the show that daren't ask questions! This week's congregation of blue-rinse biddies comes live from Golgotha.

■ ■ ■ *Bible rating: Clap–happy!*

4.30 ORDINATION STREET: The everyday encounters of folk in the priesthood. In tonight's episode the monks have a quiet night in studying, while Father O'Malley prepares for the Eucharist.

■ ■ ■ *Bible rating: Gripping church soap.*

BIBLE

4.50 SURPRISE SUR-PRISE: The heart-warming show that reunites long losts relatives and distant seeds in front of the cameras – then films them all wailing and gnashing their teeth.

5.20 CARRY ON SODOM AND GOMORRAH: more corny comedy capers with the God-fearing gang

6.00 SIX O'CLOCK GOOD NEWS with Martin Lewis. Happy tales from the Holy Land. Tonight, the blind man who can see and the cat who survived Sodom.
■ ■ ■ *Bible rating: Makes yer feel good!*

7.00 WEATHER AND LOCAL PLAGUE UPDATE.

7.10 PICK OF THE MEEK: the show where the poor get the chance to speak out.

8.00 DISPATCHES: "It's Not True." Typical! Just when we've all been converted, along come Channel 4 and ruin it all by dig-ging up documents in the Dead Sea which suggest the whole New Testament is nonsense!
■ ■ ■ *Bible rating: Spoilsports!*

8.50 ROUGH JUSTICE: New evidence sug-gests that Cane may not have been responsible for the death of his brother, Abel, and that his confession – wit-nessed only by God – may have been made under pres-sure.
■ ■ ■ *Bible rating: Courtroom conundrum!*

9.30 CRIMEWATCH AD: Bible readers are invited to piece together more real life Testament tragedies. Who is behind the bullrush child–snatch gang? And were you among the crowd that shouted for Barabus?
■ ■ ■ *Bible rating:*

R e a l – l i f e crime–busting!

10.00 EQUINOX: "The world is round." More boat-rocking from Channel 4 with claims that the world may not be flat.

11.00 THE LATE SHOW: Highbrow Hebrews and Bible boffins fight over tiny differ-ences in their beliefs.
■ ■ ■ *Bible rating: Does your head in.*

12.00 "JERICHO": Late night Hollywood dis-aster movie in which Charlton Heston plays John the Bap-tist and tries to save Jesus from the evil clutches of Pharaoh – but ends up finding love in the arms of Eve!
■ ■ ■ *Bible rating: Anything's possible in The Bible.*

The last elevenses

DOUGH THIS IN REMEMBRANCE OF ME

MORBID MESSIAH BIDS A FONDUE FAREWELL AT FINAL PRIEST FEAST

JESUS and his pupil pals gathered for a farewell feast last night that was fit for a King of the Jews.

All expenses were spared for the meagre menu which merely consisted of bread and wine.

Hannibal

But before the disciples could complain, Jezza explained the

By BIBLE REPORTER

symbolic importance of his messianic morsels.

"This is the body of Christ," he mumbled as he took a mouthful. "Do this in remembrance of me."

And the disciples could only swap odd looks when he washed it down with wine and gargled, "Likewise, this is the blood of Christ."

Dracula

But the Saviour's slap-up took a depressing turn when the Messiah grew morbid and predicted his betrayal and death.

The disciples, however, would not be downhearted and sang hymns until late into the night.

"Que Sahara, Sahara!" they were heard to holler as they rolled up the Mount of Olives. "We're going to Gethsemane."

Rave in  *the Nave*

BY PIERCED ORGAN

Security says 'NO' but I get disciples into top bash

Mates with the Messiah

Buddies with the Buddha

Mucking around with Mohammed

WHAT A CHEEK!

By BIBLE REPORTER

DOUBLE-CROSSING devotee Judas Iscariot sneaked on his Saviour for 30 pieces of silver - *and then kissed him on the cheek!*

The dirty deed that could spell doom for the Divine One was clinched after Judas held a secret meeting with top church chiefs.

He agreed to lead them to the Garden of Gethsemane where Jesus was chatting to his chaplain chums.

Kiss and tell

And he fingered his former friend by planting a sultry smacker on the Chosen One's cheek.

"Kiss me quick," was Jesus' frosty reply as the guards put him under arrest.

"You have the right to remain silent," one told him.

"But anything you say may be taken down and used in evidence."

"Those who live by the sword shall die by the sword," offered Jesus as they led him away to spend a night in the slammer.

"We're with you in spirit!" shouted the disciples, as they deserted their Messianic mate and fled to the hills.

SOUNDBITES OF THE SAVIOUR

"DO NOT throw your pearls in front of pigs - they will only trample them underfoot."
(Matt. 7:6)

"THE KINGDOM of heaven is like unto leaven which a woman took, and hid in three measures of meal till the whole was leavened."
(Matt. 13:33)

Do you know what Jesus is on about? We haven't got a clue either! Write and tell us what *you* think is going on inside the weird mind of the Messiah . Write to:
Cryptic Christ, The Bible, PO Box 21,
The Promised Land

"Let not thy left hand know what thy right hand doeth."
(Matt 6:3)

"For do not be afraid - you are worth much more than many sparrows."
(Matt. 10:31)

"Every teacher of the Law who becomes a disciple in the Kingdom of heaven is like the owner of a house who takes new and old things out of his storeroom."
(Matt. 13:52)

HANG ABOUT

BACK-STABBING believer Judas tried to make up for his Messianic misdmeanour by handing back the blood money after Jesus' arrest.

But the too-late turn-around was met with jeers from the finger-pointing Pharisees.

And the down-in-the-mouth disciple was left so depressed he decided to hang himself from a tree.

A note found at his feet said simply "Someone had to do it - it was written by the prophet Isaiah."

HE'S THE MAN WE LOVE TO HATE – READ THE JUDAS DIARIES NEXT WEEK IN YOUR No.1 BIBLE

"He's discovered they were 30 pieces of Ratner's silver."

TEN OTHER THINGS YOU COULD DO FOR 30 PIECES OF SILVER - SEE BIBLE MONEY

NAY! NAY! AND THRICE NAY!

PETRIFIED Peter has denied being a mate of the Messiah - in a bid to save his own skin.

The panicking apostle turned his back on Jesus after being picked out **three times** by servant girls and passers-by.

They insisted that they recognised Peter as a chum of the Chosen One.

By BIBLE REPORTER

But Peter denied even ever meeting Jesus!

And the fibbing follower faced further humiliation when his treachery was pointed out by a crowing cock.

"He went out and wept bitterly," disclosed a disciple insider.

THERE'S ONLY ONE GOD - AND HE'S OURS!. SO YOU MIGHT AS WELL REJOICE 'COS YOU'VE GOT NO CHOICE!

God's No1 Son always reads the Bible

YOU'VE BEEN FRAMED

Jesus to be sentenced by Pontius Pilate on Friday

DIVINE DETAINEE Jesus of Nazareth faced a kangaroo court yesterday as Pharisees and church chiefs conspired to cook up a catalogue of trumped-up charges.

Bogus witnesses and false prophets all lined up to tell porkie pies about the pious plaintiff.

One even told how Jesus had boasted he could blow up a temple and build it again in three days *single-handed*.

But Jesus kept them guessing "and held his peace".

It looked as if a not-

By BIBLE REPORTER

guilty verdict was on the cards when the priestly prosecution piped-up with a charge that no-fibbing Jesus could never deny:

"Are you the Messiah, the Son of God?"

"So you say," he replied, and annoyed them all by adding that they might as well get on and have him killed - because it was already written by the prophet Isaiah.

That was enough to seal the Saviour's fate and the fuming Pharisees charged him with blasphemy, encouraging tax evasion, and calling himself king.

Join the Church of England
YOU ONLY HAVE TO GO TWICE A YEAR!

Some religions make you pray three times a day, avoid meat, sport strange haircuts, and flagellate yourself in times of grief. But with the C of E salvation comes free! Simply turn up at Christmas and Easter – and you too will get to heaven before you can say "Nunc Dimitis"!

WASH 'N' GO

Pilate passes the buck and sets off Messianic mix-up

A FEW FLIPPANT remarks from Pontius Pilate was all it took to seal it for the Saviour.

For just as Jesus looked like getting off the hook, a crowd of pissed-up party-goers demanded he be crucified instead of convicted crook Barabbas!

Roman prelate Pontius Pilate couldn't find fault with the set-up Saviour, but top priests and scripture boffins insisted he was guilty.

So probing Pilate appealed to the people of Jerusalem who were all in the middle of a Passover party. As a goodwill gift

By BIBLE REPORTER

he promised to free the prisoner of their choice.

But a selection of heckling Hebrews - hand-picked by the Pharisees - made sure the decision went Barabbas' way.

"Free Barabbas and crucify Jesus!" was the unanimous cry of the people's poll.

But sheepish Pilate didn't feel at all easy with the outcome so he washed his hands before the crowd, saying, "I am innocent of the blood of this just person, see ye to it."

"That's all right," cheered the gleeful gathering. "His blood be on us, and on our children!"

It was a bleak day for mankind and a depressing result for campaigners of the Nazareth One.

NAILED

IT CERTAINLY wasn't a Good Friday as far as Jesus was concerned.

It started with a mammoth mocking from rowdy Roman guards and finished on a cross being jeered by frenzied Pharisees.

After a night in the slammer the Saviour woke up to find himself surrounded by a gloating garrison.

In a tirade of teasing torture they:

● **DRESSED** him up in a purple robe and crown of thorns

● **FORCED** him to drink vinegar

● **HAILED** him as King of the Jews!

Then the ghastly guards frogmarched the Messiah up a hill and nailed him to a cross.

But the baiting didn't stop there. They tore the Saviour's smock to shreds and handed them out as sick souvenirs! Then chief priests, scribes, and even elders all joined in to harass the Holy One.

"If you're so clever you can save *yourself*!" sniggered one Saducee.

But throughout his ordeal the prophet stayed placid. It was a fine display of determined divinity and only once did he cry out in ancient Hebrew:

"Dad! Forgive them - they haven't got a clue what they're doing!"

But the last laugh was on mankind, for just as the Saviour slipped away:

● **THE** veil of a temple was rent in two

● **THE** earth quaked
● **THE** rocks also did rent
● **GRAVES** split open
● **DEAD** saints jumped out of their tombs and ran amok.

"He was the Son of God alright!" gasped a gob-smacked guard. "It was like Halloween out there."

Christianity

IN CRISIS

RISE AND SHINE

Panic as prophet goes walkabout

YOU CAN'T keep a good prophet down. And Jesus is no exception!

Just when he's been written off as dead and buried for three days, stone us if he doesn't rise again!

The Saviour had been sealed in a solid stone tomb by his downcast dad Joseph.

Open Sesame!

But faffing Pharisees insisted soldiers should stand sentry too - in case their prize catch be plundered by a ghoulish gang of body-snatching believers.

But the guards could only

By BIBLE REPORTER

grovel when an angel of the Lord flew in and sparked a massive earthquake. Then the Holy Ghost heaved the giant boulder away from the door "and sat upon it!"

The shocking scenes were witnessed by former-virgin Mary and her holy hooker pal "toe-job" Mary - who'd

both turned up to mourn the Messiah.

But imagine their surprise when Christ's crypt turned out to be empty and Houdini Hebrew Jesus had already done a runner.

"Fear not!" cheered the cherub. "For he has risen!"

And he told them to go forth and round up the disciples for a religious reunion at Galilee.

"Honest sarge, he was here a minute ago."

"Now that's what I call unlucky."

JESUS LIVES!

★ Since the Saviour's tragic "death" thousands of you have written in fuelling rumours that he might have been "resurrected". Others have told of chance meetings, bleeding palms, and Jesus-shaped clouds! Here's a headline round-up of your Saviour sightings - but keep 'em coming - there's half a dinarii for those we print. Write to: *Second Coming, The Bible, PO Box 21, Bethlehem.*

JESUS SAVED FROM TOMB BY ELVIS

Second comer is local plumber

NEW MESSIAH IS CHIP FRYER

JESUS FOUND ON MOON IN DOUBLE-DECKER BUS

WINE STAIN FACE OF JESUS ON BOTTOM OF MY GOURD

CAT PEED ON MY CARPET

COULD THIS BE THE URINE SHROUD?

Rise again ...
bungee jumping
Jehovah

IS IT A BIRD? IS IT A PLANE? NO – IT'S A SOARAWAY SAVIOUR!

ASTONISHED APOSTLES have told how they "watched in wonder" as the Saviour defied gravity and skimmed through the sky.

Although technically dead, the zooming zombie turned up on a mountain outside Bethany to give his disciples their final orders.

But just as he was telling them all to "Go preach!" he suddenly began to hover on the hillside.

With a single leap the levitating Lord was taken up! up! and away!

By BIBLE REPORTER

It was pure showmanship to the last - and a smashing way for the Messiah to end his ministry.

"Missing you already!" called his apostle pals as the Saviour straddled the stratosphere.

THE BIBLE SAYS ...

JESUS is off! And who can blame him?

Recession. Romans, and fringe religions – it's enough to make you weep and wail.

Who'd want to stay here in a god-forsaken place like this –*with us for followers.*

God knows when there'll be a second coming. But let's hope it's soon!

10 THINGS YOU NEED TO KNOW ABOUT THE FUTURE

1 **FOUR** hideous horsemen will ride roughshod round the world bringing war, famine, disease and death to all. Only 144,000 souls will be set aside for salvation by Jesus who will be cunningly disguised as a lamb.

2 **IRATE** angels will then pelt our planet with fire, blood, shooting stars and anything else they can get their hands on!

3 **AND** we won't be thrilled to blitz when one of the cursed comets blows open a bottomless pit and lets loose a plague of cross-dressing locusts with the faces of men and the hair of women. They will rule the world for five months by shunning shrubberies and munching only on men. Apparently, we'll all wish we were dead, but not be able to die!

4 **THERE'LL** be more wailing and gnashing of teeth when a third of what's left of mankind gets wiped out by a herd of head-hunting horsemen.

5 **RANDOM** earthquakes, storms, slayings, plagues, bottomless pits and assorted New Testament nasties will follow hard on their heels.

6 **THINGS** will look even more bleak when Satan gets hurled out of heaven and hailed as King by hordes of hoodwinked Hebrews.

7 **YOU** must avoid him like the plague if you want to get saved. And dressed as a giant seven-headed, ten-horned, red dragon with 42 mouths, he shouldn't be hard to miss. (But if you're still not sure, check for a "666" shaped birthmark on his brow.)

8 **EVIL** men everywhere will be "gnawing their tongues in pain" as the almighty Lamb of God unleashes a heavenly hurricane on the hopeless heretics.

9 **THEN** a hairy whore will ride into view sprayed in purple, drinking the blood of saints and sitting astride a "scarlet beast". She'll be "filthy with fornication" - but you can ignore her because she's just a metaphor.

10 **CUMBAYA** my Lord! Jesus Christ will come again in his terrifying "lamb" guise and give Satan the kicking he so richly deserves. Then earth will be turned into heaven and we'll all live happily ever after. (Well, 144,000 of us at any rate.)

But don't panic. It could be worse

10 THINGS THAT MIGHT HAPPEN INSTEAD

1 **THE** faith will fragment into thousands of splinter groups. All will proclaim each other the "infidel" and millions of people will die in the name of religion.

2 **NEW** religions will join in - and although they share many of the same scriptures - the next two thousand odd years will be spent raping, pillaging and burning hated heretics everywhere.

3 **A SO-CALLED** "New World" will be discovered and its inoffensive natives will be enslaved, butchered and robbed - all in the name of God!

4 **ABOUT** the same time - a syphilis-ridden king will boost his bank balance by stealing the church's wealth and changing religions. A new faith will be formed - called "The Church of England".

5 **AN** astronomer will be locked up for life by the "Catholic" church because of his irritating insistence that the Earth is the centre of the universe.

6 **LATER**, a man of learning will be rightly ridiculed for his potty proposal that we are are descended from monkeys and *not* Adam and Eve after all!

7 **THEN** men calling themselves "missionaries" will cross the four corners of the globe to hoax, coax and bribe their way into the homes of harmless heathens.

8 **SCROLLS** will be found in cave on the Dead Sea that suggest the New Testament may not be all true - and the church shall hide them from the eyes of sinners.

9 **THERE** *won't* be a Second Coming - though thousands will stay up all night waiting, and others will claim that they are He.

10 **BUT** there *will* be an Armageddon! And as the world sinks into a cesspool of mankind's own making millions of people will be killed in the name of religion. Meanwhile the church will wind itself up over women priests.

"I think it's about time we
gave up religion and got back to God"

–*Lenny Bruce*